THE ARMOR
OF GOD

8 STUDIES FOR INDIVIDUALS OR GROUPS

Life Guide®
BIBLE STUDIES

DOUGLAS CONNELLY

IVP
Bible
Studies

An imprint of InterVarsity Press
Downers Grove, Illinois

InterVarsity Press
P.O. Box 1400 | Downers Grove, IL 60515-1426
ivpress.com | email@ivpress.com

InterVarsity Press® is the publishing division of InterVarsity Christian Fellowship/USA®. For more information, visit www.intervarsity.org.

All Scripture quotations, unless otherwise indicated, are taken from The Holy Bible, New International Version®, NIV®. Copyright © 1973, 1978, 1984, 2011 by Biblica, Inc.™ Used by permission of Zondervan. All rights reserved worldwide. www.zondervan.com. The "NIV" and "New International Version" are trademarks registered in the United States Patent and Trademark Office by Biblica, Inc.™

While any stories in this book are true, some names and identifying information may have been changed to protect the privacy of individuals.

The publisher cannot verify the accuracy or functionality of website URLs used in this book beyond the date of publication.

Cover design: Anna Poel
Interior design: Jeanna Wiggins
Images: ©idrisen / iStock / Getty Images Plus

ISBN 978-1-5140-0811-9 (print) | ISBN 978-1-5140-0812-6 (digital)

Printed in the United States of America ∞

30   29   28   27   26   25   24 | 12   11   10   9   8   7   6   5   4   3   2   1

CONTENTS

GETTING THE MOST OUT OF
THE ARMOR OF GOD

Most of the time we have other things on our minds. We're thinking about paying the mortgage or picking up the kids or replacing the tires on the car. We don't realize that a battle is going on all around us in a realm we cannot see but that is just as real as the realm of mortgages and kids and tires. The battle is between those of us who are followers of Jesus and incredible evil beings who are seeking to discourage and defeat us in our spiritual life.

Spiritual warfare is very real—and very personal. Our spiritual enemy, Satan, is a roaring lion, a deceiving spirit, and a habitual liar. He will use any tactic to turn us away from faithful, joyful obedience to Jesus. He laughs at the commitments we make to live in this world as a loving spouse or as a devoted parent or as a courageous disciple. He will do anything he can to keep us from consistent time in prayer or in the study of God's Word or from setting a godly example for people who are influenced by us. Satan is always on the attack!

The avenue to counter his attacks is to be awake to his schemes—and to prepare ourselves for the battle. In Ephesians 6 the apostle Paul gives us the clearest description anywhere in Scripture of the resources that are available to us in the spiritual battle. In this letter Paul is speaking to the church at Ephesus as these early Christians faced persecution. He describes spiritual resources as armor provided by God for our defense and for the Christian community. It's not literal armor we can order online; it's spiritual armor that we take up each day, each moment, for the spiritual war that rages around us and against us.

In these studies we will discover not only what our resources are but also how to put on the armor and how to rely on God's provision when the enemy comes against us. We can be confident that Christ rules over all authorities, and *the same power that raised Jesus from the dead is at work in us* (Ephesians 1:18-23). Victory over God's enemies is already secured.

Still, Satan and the evil powers under his control do not want you to choose this study or to complete its sections. After all, you might take what God says to heart and become far more effective in deflecting Satan's attacks in your life! But if you faithfully put on each piece of armor and overcome Satan's opposition, you will find yourself fully equipped to face whatever the enemy throws at you.

SUGGESTIONS FOR INDIVIDUAL STUDY

1. As you begin each study, pray that God will speak to you through his Word.

2. Read the introduction to the study and respond to the personal reflection question or exercise. This is designed to help you focus on God and on the theme of the study.

3. Each study deals with a particular passage so that you can delve into the author's meaning in that context. Read and reread the passage to be studied. The questions are written using the language of the New International Version, so you may wish to use that version of the Bible. The New Revised Standard Version is also recommended.

4. This is an inductive Bible study, designed to help you discover for yourself what Scripture is saying. The study includes three types of questions. *Observation* questions ask about the basic facts: who, what, when, where, and how. *Interpretation* questions delve into the meaning of the passage. *Application* questions help you discover the implications of the text for growing in Christ. These three keys unlock the treasures of Scripture.

Write your answers to the questions in the spaces provided or in a personal journal. Writing can bring clarity and deeper understanding of yourself and of God's Word.

5. It might be good to have a Bible dictionary handy. Use it to look up any unfamiliar words, names, or places.

6. Use the prayer suggestion to guide you in thanking God for what you have learned and to pray about the applications that have come to mind.

7. You may want to go on to the suggestion under "Now or Later," or you may want to use that idea for your next study.

SUGGESTIONS FOR MEMBERS OF A GROUP STUDY

1. Come to the study prepared. Follow the suggestions for individual study mentioned above. You will find that careful preparation will greatly enrich your time spent in group discussion.

2. Be willing to participate in the discussion. The leader of your group will not be lecturing. Instead, he or she will be encouraging the members of the group to discuss what they have learned. The leader will be asking the questions that are found in this guide.

3. Stick to the topic being discussed. Your answers should be based on the verses which are the focus of the discussion and not on outside authorities such as commentaries or speakers. These studies focus on a particular passage of Scripture. Only rarely should you refer to other portions of the Bible. This allows for everyone to participate in in-depth study on equal ground.

4. Be sensitive to the other members of the group. Listen attentively when they describe what they have learned. You may be surprised by their insights! Each question assumes a variety of answers. Many questions do not have "right" answers, particularly questions that aim at meaning or application. Instead the questions push us to explore the passage more thoroughly.

When possible, link what you say to the comments of others. Also, be affirming whenever you can. This will encourage some of the more hesitant members of the group to participate.

5. Be careful not to dominate the discussion. We are sometimes so eager to express our thoughts that we leave too little opportunity for others to respond. By all means participate! But allow others to also.

6. Expect God to teach you through the passage being discussed and through the other members of the group. Pray that you will have an enjoyable and profitable time together, but also that as a result of the study you will find ways that you can take action individually and/or as a group.

7. Remember that anything said in the group is considered confidential and should not be discussed outside the group unless specific permission is given to do so.

8. If you are the group leader, you will find additional suggestions at the back of the guide.

ONE

BE STRONG: THE BATTLE AGAINST US

Ephesians 6:10-13

One of the most powerful confrontations with evil I have ever experienced took place in the foyer of a church! As the pastor, I was greeting people as they balanced coffee cups and Bibles when I noticed the entrance of a young woman who occasionally attended the church. Behind her was a man I had never met, but I immediately sensed a strong warning in my mind and spirit. I made my way over to the couple and introduced myself. The man was a new boyfriend, and it was obvious that he was not happy to be in church. The uneasiness in my spirit only grew stronger as I talked briefly with them and then moved on.

When I went into the sanctuary for the service, I prayed silently that God would keep whatever evil power had entered our building from having any influence in our worship that morning. As I prayed, the unease in me began to disappear, and we went on with the worship service as normal. I had almost forgotten about the man as I preached that Sunday, but about ten minutes into the message, he stood up and walked out. The spirit in him could not tolerate the Spirit in our church body, and he left. Sadly, he never came back.

Group Discussion. How would you explain what the author sensed that Sunday? What do you think of his response?

Personal Reflection. Have you ever had a similar experience when you sensed the presence of evil? How did you or would you react?

The Bible makes it clear that a battle is going on in the spiritual realm between God and Satan—between spiritual powers of good and truth and spiritual powers of darkness and evil. That battle includes those of us who are Christians, followers of Jesus. We are the target of these evil powers. They try every way they can to defeat, deceive, and discourage us. The apostle Paul issues a strong warning about the battle—and we ignore that warning to our own peril. *Read Ephesians 6:10-13.*

1. How familiar are you with the idea of a spiritual battle, and what is your reaction to what Paul says in this Scripture?

2. The spiritual forces arrayed against us as believers seem almost overwhelming at times. List all the words in verse 12 that speak of power.

3. While we may feel powerless and pinned down at times, we are not alone in the battle. We have a relationship with someone who is far greater than all our enemies—and he has committed himself to rescue us! What words or phrases in verses 10-13 speak to you of God's overcoming power?

| What point do you think Paul intends to make with this list?

4. Name a difficult problem or relationship you are facing right now. Explain how you have struggled with the situation up to this point.

5. Think about the possibility that there might be a spiritual dimension to your problem. You may be wrestling with emotional, financial, or physical issues, but the true enemy is behind the scenes: the devil and the evil forces under his direction. What might be the goal of the spiritual forces of evil in your specific situation?

6. The word *schemes* in verse 11 suggests a well-thought-out strategy for victory. Satan and the powers under his control have a plan for your life—and it's not good! What would you identify as your own areas of greatest vulnerability and weakness?

7. How does awareness of spiritual conflict affect how you view your current problems and how you might respond to them?

8. Paul's command to "be strong in the Lord" (v. 10) is a passive verb in Paul's Greek language. It means that this strength is something God gives and we receive. What are some ways you can receive strength from the Lord?

9. Victory in our spiritual battles is not automatic. We too have a part to play in the conflict. What are we called to do in verses 10-13?

10. Armor Assessment. Military friends tell me that every day before going out on their assigned mission, a service member conducts an assessment of their protective body armor and weapons to make sure they are ready to face what lies ahead. As part of each study, we will conduct a spiritual armor assessment.

The command to "put on the full armor of God" is an active command—something we do. There is also a sense of urgency in the command. How would you describe the importance to you of putting on the armor of God?

11. How will this study affect the way you pray about problems or difficult relationships in your life?

Thank God that the victory belongs to him. Pray for God's help to take up the armor he has provided.

NOW OR LATER

Read 2 Corinthians 10:3-5. How does this passage fit with what you read in Ephesians 6? What does it suggest to you about the kind of fighting Christians are called to?

TWO

STAY TRUE: THE BELT OF TRUTH

Ephesians 6:13-17; 2 Timothy 3:10-17

F itness gyms have sprouted throughout my community. Many of them are open twenty-four hours a day. At any time, from early in the morning until late at night, I see men and women trudging in and out, working to strengthen their bodies or to shed a few pounds or to keep their heart and lungs functioning well.

Most personal trainers or fitness gurus want their clients to focus on strengthening their *core*—the area of the abdomen, back, and pelvis that provides a solid foundation for any other kind of physical workout. A strong core contributes to good balance and stability and keeps a person in control of their entire body.

Group Discussion. What do you like (or dislike) about exercise? What do most people hope to gain from fitness training?

Personal Reflection. What is your spiritual core like? What are some places where you are experiencing stability or shakiness, strength or weakness, balance or imbalance in your life?

Paul bases his imagery of our spiritual armor on the uniform worn by a Roman soldier. The first readers of Paul's letters would have seen Roman soldiers every day, like police officers in our culture.

The first piece of armor stabilized the soldier's core—the seat of his strength and agility. He had his "loins girded" (ASV) with a wide leather belt that buckled snugly around his midsection. Think about the wide belt an Olympic weight lifter wears to provide support for heavy lifting. The Ephesians 6 belt serves the same purpose. It provides essential support for the demanding tasks of work and warfare. *Read Ephesians 6:13-17.*

1. The pieces of armor are listed in Ephesians 6 in the same order that a soldier would put them on to prepare for battle (vv. 14-17). Make a list of the pieces in order. Think about how each would look. Do an internet search for each piece of the armor or try to draw the armor. (Don't worry, it's for your eyes only!)

2. The belt in our spiritual armor is truth. How does truth act in our lives like the belt in the Roman soldier's life?

3. How would you describe the world's view of truth that's dominant in your context?

4. What is your view of truth as a follower of Christ?

5. If truth is the essential foundation of our protection in the spiritual battle, what does this tell you about how the enemy may seek to attack you?

6. What steps can you take to be more grounded in God's truth and to live that truth more faithfully?

Read 2 Timothy 3:10-17.
7. What does Paul say about knowing and believing God's truth?

What does he say about living out that truth?

8. What is the truth of Scripture useful for (vv. 16-17)?

9. Describe how you are passing the truth along to others, or explain what may be holding you back.

10. Armor Assessment. The belt helped the Roman soldier stand straighter and carry a heavy load more comfortably. (A soldier's armor and supplies could weigh about sixty pounds!) The belt of truth has the same function for us spiritually. By buckling on the belt of truth, we are enabled to stand more firmly in our faith and to carry the burdens of life more comfortably. What resources for discovering God's truth do you most often draw on?

11. What can you begin to do today to prompt yourself to turn more quickly to God's truth in time of attack or need?

Praise God that he is true and that we can trust who he is and what he says. Pray that you can be faithful to build your life on the truth.

NOW OR LATER

Psalm 119 is a long meditation on the power of God's Word. Read it slowly and reflectively. Maybe read it out loud. Mark the verses that speak most directly to you of the importance of God's truth in your life. Copy some of the verses into a journal or on small cards. Use the cards to help you memorize a few of the passages.

THREE

BE ON GUARD: THE BREASTPLATE OF RIGHTEOUSNESS

Ephesians 6:14; 1 Corinthians 16:10-14

My friend Jason Chew had to wear an IOTV (improved outer tactical vest) every day while he was stationed in Afghanistan. It weighed between twenty and thirty pounds, but he did not need to be reminded to put on his vest. He knew that in a war zone the battle could come at any time. Every soldier knew that what seemed cumbersome and heavy at times could save their life if they were attacked. Jason said that when a person put the vest on every day, they got used to it. It was part of their uniform. No one would think of leaving on a mission without it.

Group Discussion. Do you feel sometimes that doing the right thing in obedience to God is cumbersome—almost an annoyance—like wearing a heavy vest? Talk about what those moments are like.

Personal Reflection. When do you feel safest, most protected? Where are you and who is around you at those times?

The next piece of armor we are called to take up is the breastplate—a heavy metal plate that covered the front and back of the body and protected vital organs like the heart, lungs, and liver. The breastplate was held in place with leather straps and hooked on to the leather belt just below it. It shielded the body from arrows and blows from a sword. Wearing the breastplate could mean the difference between life and death. The early church father Jerome said, "One who has put on a sturdy breastplate is difficult to wound."* *Read Ephesians 6:14.*

1. What is the breastplate made of in this passage?

What image does a "breastplate of righteousness" evoke for you?

2. The Bible uses the word *righteousness* in two ways. First, we have the righteousness of Christ given to us by God's grace when we believe in Jesus as Savior and Lord. We are in a right relationship with God because the penalty of our sin was paid in full on the cross. The second kind of righteousness comes as we live rightly before God and the world. It doesn't save us, but it reflects God's character and demonstrates our obedience to God's Word. Reflecting on this, what do you think the breastplate of righteousness is meant to symbolize?

3. How might the devil and the evil forces under his control try to attack your vital organs—your heart, your spirit, your emotions, your ambitions, your attitudes—as a Christian?

4. Think of a time in your life when you were not living according to God's design and you fell into one of Satan's traps of discouragement, deception, or sinful behavior. How did you get back to a better place?

5. Followers of Jesus should have an awareness of living under the protection of Christ's righteousness given to us by God's grace. What effect does this truth have on your daily battle with evil?

Read 1 Corinthians 16:10-14.

6. In this section of his letter to the Corinthians, Paul is making some specific requests and sharing his plans. What requests does he make in regard to Timothy?

7. What four commands does Paul give to those who seek to live righteously in a world system that opposes them (v. 13)?

Rewrite the commands in your own words, inserting your own name into them.

8. Which of these commands do you most need to hear today and why?

9. Now focus on the command in verse 14. How does it expand the meaning of the other commands?

10. Armor Assessment. At times, ancient armor was adorned with a symbol. What symbol or design would you put on the breastplate of righteousness that God offers to you and why?

11. Does it make you feel more vulnerable or more protected when you realize that God's breastplate covers your innermost thoughts, feelings, and desires? Explain.

12. Every day we are called to pursue right living as we face the world. We don't strive for perfection (an impossible quest) but a life that pleases the Lord. What can you do to remind yourself to consciously, intentionally seek right living each day?

Give thanks for the promise of righteousness, that is, having a right relationship with God, because of Jesus' sacrifice on the cross. Pray for the willingness to live outwardly what God has declared us to be.

NOW OR LATER

The Lord is often pictured in the Old Testament as a divine warrior. Isaiah 59:15-19 is one passage that describes him that way, and it forms the background for the armor of God in Ephesians 6. Read Isaiah's words. Then read the passage again and identify the parallels with Ephesians 6 that you discover there. Do not miss the powerful teaching of the passage: our armor is the Lord's own armor, provided to us as a gift and empowered by the Spirit to ensure our victory.

---

*Jerome, *Epistle to the Ephesians* 3.6.14.

FOUR

STAND FIRM: FEET
FITTED WITH READINESS

Ephesians 6:14-15; Romans 5:1-5

No **Bible story** is more exciting than the account of David in battle with Goliath. David was a young shepherd filled with zeal for the Lord God; Goliath is traditionally believed to have been a nine-and-a-half-foot thug, ready to fight anyone foolish enough to step from the ranks of the army of Israel. In addition to his size and strength, Goliath was sheathed in a full set of armor. Most people thought that if David was to have a fighting chance, he needed armor too.

David tried King Saul's armor, but it was too bulky and heavy. Instead, David chose a sling and five smooth stones—and put his confidence in the Lord God of Israel. The battle was quick and ended with a very surprised Philistine army! David won the victory that day because he chose the armor and the weapons suitable for his unique enemy.

Group Discussion. What are your favorite shoes, and when do you wear them?

Personal Reflection. What kind of spiritual shoes do you think you're wearing right now? High, clunky heels? Ratty tennis shoes? Expensive trail boots? Are you standing firm or are you slipping?

The third piece of armor followers of Jesus are called to put on are the war boots. For the Roman soldier, a war boot was a sturdy, open-toed leather sandal with a nail-studded sole. (Think of a cleated football shoe.) The sandal was tied to the ankle and lower leg with long leather straps. Those who are called to stand their ground need to have secure footing. *Read Ephesians 6:14-15.*

1. Once followers of Jesus are clothed with the belt of truth and the breastplate of righteousness, Paul admonishes us to stand firm. According to him, what allows us to do this?

2. This is the only place where Paul refers to the "gospel of peace." What do you think the significance is in the context of these verses?

3. How can a Christian have peace in the middle of a battle?

4. In what ways or areas of life does the enemy rob you of peace?

5. How do you normally handle situations or feelings of disharmony or unrest, and what is the outcome?

6. The shoes were studded to help the Roman soldier move over difficult or slick terrain. What does that tell you about following Jesus into the spiritual battle?

7. Armor Assessment. Soldiers need to pay close attention to the quality of their footwear—their lives may depend on it. What are your war boots like: beat up and broken down, or prepared for whatever lies ahead? Are your feet prepared to stand firm in the battle and then to move ahead confidently? Check what you are wearing and ask God to help you be prepared and alert, ready for the terrain in front of you.

8. What motivates you to share the message of how to have peace with God, or what holds you back?

Read Romans 5:1-5.
9. What results are produced in our lives because we are justified by faith in Jesus?

10. What are the outcomes of suffering according to verses 3-4?

11. Suffering and facing battles usually feel like the most difficult ways to grow. What does it mean for us to "glory in our sufferings"?

12. We don't usually think of our feet as beautiful, and yet the prophet Isaiah wrote, "How beautiful on the mountains are the feet of those who bring good news, who proclaim peace" (Isaiah 52:7). Into what situation or relationship can you speak or bring peace this week?

Pray that you and the people close to you will know the peace of God and leave footprints of peace wherever you go.

NOW OR LATER

Sometimes attaching a spiritual discipline to an everyday responsibility helps us develop good spiritual habits. Why not try this: when you put on your shoes every morning, think about also tying on the shoes of the gospel of peace. Put on God's armor as you put on your clothes! Do it for a week—intentionally, deliberately—and then tell a friend or your study group how it went.

FIVE

STAY CONFIDENT: THE SHIELD OF FAITH

Ephesians 6:16; Psalm 18:6-30

Why am I so surprised when God does something that he has promised to do? Or, to use Jesus' words, "Why is it that *you* of all people have no faith?" (Mark 4:40, my paraphrase). After all, I am a pastor! I call on people all the time to trust God and his promises. When I visit someone who is discouraged or lonely, I ask them to remember the faithful character of God and his promise never to abandon us as his children. When I pray for a person in the hospital who has a terminal diagnosis and I ask God for a work of his healing power, why am I stunned to see that person walk into a worship service a few weeks later? I find myself praying an unnamed father's prayer more often than I like to admit: "I do believe; help me overcome my unbelief!" (Mark 9:24).

Group Discussion. Is there something today that is causing you to struggle to believe God's promises or to rest in God's faithfulness? What or who usually helps you through those times of doubt?

Personal Reflection. Can you recall a recent time when God amazed you by answering your prayer or fulfilling one of his promises in your life? Write it down. Who can you encourage with this story?

The first three elements of the armor of God—the belt, the breastplate, and the war boots—were foundational items worn at all times. The next three pieces—the shield, the helmet, and the sword—were kept near at hand and taken up when the enemy approached. *Read Ephesians 6:16.*

1. What does the shield of faith do?

2. Picture a flaming arrow from the evil one coming toward you. What images, thoughts, and feelings does this evoke?

3. How would you describe what the shield of faith is?

4. James says, "Faith without deeds is useless" (James 2:20). Living faith is not just talking about what we believe God is able to do; it is also translating the promises of God into action. What is a current situation or relationship in your life you believe God will work in?

5. How can you translate what you believe about that situation or relationship into action?

6. How might you encourage a struggling friend to exercise faith in a difficult circumstance?

Read Psalm 18:6-30.
7. Describe God's actions when the psalmist cries for help.

8. Have you ever watched God shoot "his arrows and scatter the enemy" (v. 14) in your life or the lives of those around you? If so, describe what that was like.

9. As you read through the Psalms passage a second time, write down words or phrases that describe what we are responsible to do and what God does or is.

Our Responsibility   God's Promises

10. What do you notice about these two lists?

11. Armor Assessment. Some Roman shields were designed to hook on to the shield of the soldier on either side. The connected shields formed a solid defensive wall against the enemy. What does that tell you about the importance of bringing other faith-filled Christians around you when you feel attacked?

12. What keeps you from reaching out to others for assistance and help?

13. Looking back through Psalm 18, what do you most need from God that you see offered in these verses?

In whatever you are struggling with today, express your belief in God and his promises. Ask God to help you overcome your unbelief.

NOW OR LATER

Make a list of areas where you sense God prompting you to take a step of faith right now. It might involve a new job, sharing the gospel with a friend, being more generous in your giving, or turning away from a habit that compromises your witness or hinders your walk with the Lord.

Why have you hesitated to move forward in those areas so far? How can you respond in obedience to the Holy Spirit now? Be specific and honest.

SIX

BE ASSURED: THE HELMET OF SALVATION

Ephesians 6:17; 1 Thessalonians 5:8-11

A s **Christians,** we sometimes think that our salvation is a one-time event sometime in the past: "I was *saved* at Bible camp when I was a teenager." It's a wonderful thing to be able to look back at the time when we responded in faith to the gospel and were transferred from the dominion of darkness into the kingdom of God's Son (Colossians 1:13).

But salvation is much broader and deeper than a one-time experience at the foot of the cross. Salvation also flows into our everyday life. We not only *have been saved* (Ephesians 2:5, 8); we *are being saved* as we grow into maturity as believers (1 Corinthians 1:18; 2 Corinthians 2:15). We were delivered from the *penalty* of sin when we believed; we are delivered from the *power* of sin as we put off the remnants of the old life and live in the realm of the Spirit as a new creation.

Even beyond that, the day will come when we will be delivered from the *presence* of sin as redeemed men and women in heaven—we *will be saved* (Mark 13:13; Romans 5:9-10).

Group Discussion. Which of these three aspects of salvation—past, present, or future—do you tend to forget or ignore most? Why?

Personal Reflection. Do you intentionally seek to "work out your salvation" (Philippians 2:12) every day—to be outwardly what God in grace has made you inwardly? How is this different from simply relying on a commitment of faith you made in the past?

The fifth piece of the armor of God is represented by the Roman soldier's helmet. Some helmets were made of thick leather, covered with metal plates; others were made entirely of metal that had been molded or beaten into shape. *Read Ephesians 6:17.*

1. What was the primary purpose of the soldier's helmet?

2. Translate that into our spiritual armor. What does this piece of armor do for the Christian?

3. Paul relates the helmet to salvation—not in the sense of coming to faith in Jesus but in the sense of the believer's confidence in salvation already received. What kind of attacks or doubts might Satan raise about our salvation and our assurance that we are saved?

4. Which of those doubts or attacks have you experienced in your mind and heart? How did you handle those struggles?

5. How would you describe a soldier who goes into battle without a helmet?

In what ways can you sometimes relate to that description?

Read 1 Thessalonians 5:8-11.
6. In these verses, what qualities does Paul associate with "putting on . . . the hope of salvation as a helmet"?

7. Which of those qualities are evident in your life, and which are lacking?

8. What responsibilities arise from being armored with the helmet of salvation (v. 11)?

9. How might you more intentionally encourage others with these truths?

10. Armor Assessment. What does your spiritual helmet look like: battered and dented from frequent use, or shiny and practically new because it sits in God's armory unused?

11. I have this statement written in the margin of my Bible at Ephesians 6:17. I'm not sure who said it or where I heard it, but it has encouraged me many times: "If you are fearful and lack confidence, reach for the helmet God has provided, pull it down hard over your head, fasten the strap, and stand tall in the battle. The victory is already assured." In what situations do you—or should you—intentionally put the helmet of salvation on?

Ask God to help you to be faithful to put on the helmet of salvation every day and to face the battle with confidence in him.

NOW OR LATER

Make a list of sporting events in which participants wear a helmet. Helmets not only provide protection; they also instill confidence. When you think of the spiritual battle around you, do you approach that battle with fear and insecurity, or does the presence of God's armor make you confident to face the enemy? How can you better display that confidence?

SEVEN

BE COURAGEOUS: THE SWORD OF THE SPIRIT

Ephesians 6:17; Hebrews 4:12-13

My grandchildren can make just about anything into a pretend weapon in their imaginary battles for world conquest. Couch pillows become bombs and flashlights become laser blasters. The latest battle was fought in our basement with long pieces of foam pipe insulation. Within seconds a massive sword fight broke out!

Group Discussion. What was your go-to pretend weapon as a child? Or what is your preferred video game weapon? How does it make you feel to be in the heat of the battle?

Personal Reflection. Have you ever had to carry a weapon for self-defense or as part of your job or in the military? How do you think you would respond to having a weapon so near all the time?

Paul's description of our spiritual armor takes a dramatic turn as he talks about the sixth piece. Up until now, the armor has been primarily defensive; it was designed to protect us from the enemy's attacks. But now Paul puts an offensive weapon in our hands, a spiritual sword!

In Paul's day this weapon was a short, one-handed sword that was carried in a leather sheath at the soldier's waist. It was ready instantly for hand-to-hand combat. *Read Ephesians 6:17.*

1. In presenting the sword, Paul mentions two defining aspects. What are these?

2. Paul explains that the sword originates from the Spirit. How might the Holy Spirit be involved in how the sword is used in our lives?

3. If we think of the sword as a spiritual weapon to be used against our spiritual enemies, in what situations would we rely on a sword?

4. Paul further explains that the sword is "the word of God." How can God's Word of truth be used as an offensive weapon to destroy and expose the enemy's schemes against us?

How can it also act as a defensive weapon to protect us?

5. Tell a story from your own experience of how God's Word protected you from temptation or harm or how you were able to resist the enemy with the sword of God's Word.

6. What are some areas of your life where you need to be on the offensive to take back ground the enemy has claimed or to overcome one of his lies that you have accepted?

7. How might you do that? What is your plan, and who can help you in carrying out that plan?

Read Hebrews 4:12-13.

8. What additional insight does this passage give you about the Word of God as a spiritual sword?

9. What does it mean to allow the Bible to penetrate your heart and mind?

10. How do you feel when you think of everything being "laid bare" (v. 13) before God?

11. Armor Assessment. A Roman soldier would be required to keep his sword ready for battle and to be ready to use the sword effectively. How would the soldier do this?

12. Using a scale of 1 to 5, evaluate your battle readiness with the sword of God's Word. Explain your evaluation.

13. What is your strategy to increase your effectiveness?

God's Word is a light on our paths, honey in our mouths, strength for our souls, and a sword in our hands. Express to God how you want to know him and his words more deeply each day.

NOW OR LATER

Write daily in a journal or notebook some of the things God speaks to you about as you read his Word. Then determine to obey what God tells you.

EIGHT

STAY DEPENDENT: PRAY!

Ephesians 6:18-20; Colossians 1:9-14

I met **Pastor Leroy** at a senior care facility in our community. I had come to visit another person but struck up a conversation with this man who was sitting in a chair in the community room. I had the privilege of talking with him several times that year. Leroy told me that during his ministry he had searched through the Bible and recorded every reference to prayer. He even knew the number of references in the Old Testament and in the New Testament. (I wish I had written that number down somewhere!)

Pastor Leroy was passionate about prayer. When I would leave, he would always ask if he could pray for me—and then he would storm heaven with a prayer for God's blessing on me and my ministry. I always left his room feeling filled with the glory of God.

Group Discussion. When do you find it easiest to pray, and when is it hardest? Why do you think that is?

Personal Reflection. Is there someone in your life who prays regularly for you? How can you express your gratitude to them?

Soldiers in the spiritual battle are dressed in the full armor of God. Every piece expresses action and readiness. The belt is firmly tightened, the breastplate is fitted exactly right, and the shoes are laced and ready to move the soldier forward. The warrior has pulled his helmet down and taken up his shield; the sword of the Spirit is in his hand. The enemy approaches and the Lord's troops are ready to stand in the attack. But then the Christian soldiers do something totally unexpected: fall to their knees in prayer! The battle will still be fought, but it will be done under the covering of prayer.

John Bunyan in *The Pilgrim's Progress* calls the seventh piece of spiritual armor "All-Prayer." Prayer is the first thing, the second thing, and the third thing—the supreme weapon available to us in the spiritual battle. *Read Ephesians 6:18-20.*

1. What phrases or words in verse 18 emphasize the priority of prayer?

Do any of these words surprise you? Why?

2. What does it mean to "pray in the Spirit"?

3. What are some of the various "prayers and requests" we might make to God?

4. Which kinds of prayer do you usually pray, and which kinds do you tend to neglect?

5. Paul also emphasizes the importance of perseverance in prayer: "always keep on praying." Do you find yourself praying once or twice for a need and then giving up? What's your perspective on this?

6. Some Christians have the idea that if we badger God often enough and hard enough, he will finally give in to our request! How would you explain why God delights in perseverance in prayer?

7. In verses 19-20 Paul asks those who read his letter to pray for him. What does Paul list as his prayer needs?

8. What spiritual leader or pastor could you begin to pray for using Paul's requests as a guideline?

Read Colossians 1:9-14.
9. Make a list of what Paul asks of God for these followers of Jesus.

10. How do the things that burden Paul's heart compare to the things you usually ask God to do in the lives of other Christians?

11. Armor Assessment. For Paul, prayer is critically important to using the armor of God. How would you evaluate your own prayer life? How has it changed over time?

12. If prayer is the first or primary thing in spiritual warfare, what specific steps can you take this week to strengthen this aspect of your spiritual armor?

Ask God to teach you to pray. Pray that in every battle, through every conversation, at every opportunity your heart turns to him.

NOW OR LATER

Write a prayer for others based on Paul's requests in Ephesians 6:19-20. Pray it regularly for a leader, pastor, or friend.

A FURTHER SUGGESTION

Once you have finished this study guide on the armor of God, carve out part of a day or go on an overnight retreat with your study group or in smaller groups of two or three. As part of the time set aside, ask the Holy Spirit to show you what your own personal armor from him looks like—not just pieces of armor in general but the armor he has prepared for you. As you wait on him in prayer, begin to describe what the Spirit brings to your mind. This is where a spiritual partner can help by writing down what you describe. Your personal armor may contain elements that are specific to the battles you are usually in. Try not to miss any aspect, no matter how small or insignificant it may seem. Use what the Spirit reveals along with Paul's description in Ephesians 6 in the days ahead as you focus on putting on and taking up the armor of God. God has designed unique armor for you! Use what he has provided by his grace to fight the spiritual battles that lie ahead.

LEADER'S NOTES

My grace is sufficient for you.

2 CORINTHIANS 12:9

L eading a Bible discussion can be an enjoyable and rewarding experience. But it can also be *scary*—especially if you've never done it before. If this is your feeling, you're in good company. When God asked Moses to lead the Israelites out of Egypt, he replied, "Lord. Please send someone else" (Exodus 4:13). It was the same with Solomon, Jeremiah, and Timothy, but God helped these people in spite of their weaknesses, and he will help you as well.

You don't need to be an expert on the Bible or a trained teacher to lead a Bible discussion. The idea behind these inductive studies is that the leader guides group members to discover for themselves what the Bible has to say. This method of learning will allow group members to remember much more of what is said than a lecture would.

These studies are designed to be led easily. As a matter of fact, the flow of questions through the passage from observation to interpretation to application is so natural that you may feel that the studies lead themselves. This study guide is also flexible. You can use it with a variety of groups—student, professional, neighborhood, or church groups. Each study takes forty-five to sixty minutes in a group setting.

There are some important facts to know about group dynamics and encouraging discussion. The suggestions listed below should enable you to effectively and enjoyably fulfill your role as leader.

PREPARING FOR THE STUDY

1. Ask God to help you understand and apply the passage in your own life. Unless this happens, you will not be prepared to lead others. Pray too for the various members of the group. Ask God to open your hearts to the message of his Word and motivate you to action.

2. Read the introduction to the entire guide to get an overview of the entire book and the issues which will be explored.

3. As you begin each study, read and reread the assigned Bible passage to familiarize yourself with it.

4. This study guide is based on the New International Version of the Bible. It will help you and the group if you use this translation as the basis for your study and discussion.

5. Carefully work through each question in the study. Spend time in meditation and reflection as you consider how to respond.

6. Write your thoughts and responses in the space provided in the study guide. This will help you to express your understanding of the passage clearly.

7. It might help to have a Bible dictionary handy. Use it to look up any unfamiliar words, names, or places. (For additional help on how to study a passage, see chapter five of *How to Lead a LifeGuide Bible Study*, InterVarsity Press.)

8. Consider how you can apply the Scripture to your life. Remember that the group will follow your lead in responding to the studies. They will not go any deeper than you do.

9. Once you have finished your own study of the passage, familiarize yourself with the leader's notes for the study you are leading. These are designed to help you in several ways. First, they tell you the purpose the study guide author had in mind when writing the study. Take time to think through how the study questions work together to accomplish that purpose. Second, the notes provide you with additional background information or suggestions on group dynamics for various questions. This information can be useful when people have difficulty understanding or answering a question. Third, the leader's notes can alert you to potential problems you may encounter during the study.

10. If you wish to remind yourself of anything mentioned in the leader's notes, make a note to yourself below that question in the study.

LEADING THE STUDY

1. Begin the study on time. Open with prayer, asking God to help the group to understand and apply the passage.

2. Be sure that everyone in your group has a study guide. Encourage the group to prepare beforehand for each discussion by reading the introduction to the guide and by working through the questions in the study.

3. At the beginning of your first time together, explain that these studies are meant to be discussions, not lectures. Encourage the members of the group to participate. However, do not put pressure on those who may be hesitant to speak during the first few sessions. You may want to suggest the following guidelines to your group:

- Stick to the topic being discussed.
- Your responses should be based on the verses which are the focus of the discussion and not on outside authorities such as commentaries or speakers.
- These studies focus on a particular passage of Scripture. Only rarely should you refer to other portions of the Bible. This allows for everyone to participate in in-depth study on equal ground.
- Anything said in the group is considered confidential and will not be discussed outside the group unless specific permission is given to do so.
- We will listen attentively to each other and provide time for each person present to talk.
- We will pray for each other.

4. Have a group member read the introduction at the beginning of the discussion.

5. Every session begins with a group discussion question. The question or activity is meant to be used before the passage is read. The question introduces the theme of the study and encourages group members to begin to open up. Encourage as many members as possible to participate, and be ready to get the discussion going with your own response.

This section is designed to reveal where our thoughts or feelings need to be transformed by Scripture. That is why it is especially important not to read the passage before the discussion question is asked. The passage will tend to color the honest reactions people would otherwise give because they are, of course, supposed to think the way the Bible does.

You may want to supplement the group discussion question with an icebreaker to help people get comfortable. See the community section of InterVarsity Press's *Small Group Idea Book* for more ideas.

You also might want to use the personal reflection question with your group. Either allow a time of silence for people to respond individually or discuss it together.

6. Have a group member (or members if the passage is long) read aloud the passage to be studied. Then give people several minutes to read the passage again silently so that they can take it all in.

7. Question 1 will generally be an overview question designed to briefly survey the passage. Encourage the group to look at the whole passage, but try to avoid getting sidetracked by questions or issues that will be addressed later in the study.

8. As you ask the questions, keep in mind that they are designed to be used just as they are written. You may simply read them aloud. Or you may prefer to express them in your own words.

There may be times when it is appropriate to deviate from the study guide. For example, a question may have already been answered. If so, move on to the next question. Or someone may raise an important question not covered in the guide. Take time to discuss it, but try to keep the group from going off on tangents.

9. Avoid answering your own questions. If necessary, repeat or rephrase them until they are clearly understood. Or point out something you read in the leader's notes to clarify the context or meaning. An eager group quickly becomes passive and silent if they think the leader will do most of the talking.

10. Don't be afraid of silence. People may need time to think about the question before formulating their answers.

11. Don't be content with just one answer. Ask, "What do the rest of you think?" or "Anything else?" until several people have given answers to the question.

12. Acknowledge all contributions. Try to be affirming whenever possible. Never reject an answer. If it is clearly off base, ask, "Which verse led you to that conclusion?" or again, "What do the rest of you think?"

13. Don't expect every answer to be addressed to you, even though this will probably happen at first. As group members become more at ease, they will begin to truly interact with each other. This is one sign of healthy discussion.

14. Don't be afraid of controversy. It can be very stimulating. If you don't resolve an issue completely, don't be frustrated. Move on and keep it in mind for later. A subsequent study may solve the problem.

15. Periodically summarize what the group has said about the passage. This helps to draw together the various ideas mentioned and gives continuity to the study. But don't preach.

16. At the end of the Bible discussion, you may want to allow group members a time of quiet to work on an idea under "Now or Later." Then discuss what you experienced. Or you may want to encourage group members to work on these ideas between meetings. Give an opportunity during the session for people to talk about what they are learning.

17. Conclude your time together with conversational prayer, adapting the prayer suggestion at the end of the study to your group. Ask for God's help in following through on the commitments you've made.

18. End on time.

Many more suggestions and helps are found in *How to Lead a LifeGuide Bible Study*, which is part of the LifeGuide Bible Study series.

COMPONENTS OF SMALL GROUPS

A healthy small group should do more than study the Bible. There are four components to consider as you structure your time together.

Nurture. Small groups help us to grow in our knowledge and love of God. Bible study is the key to making this happen and is the foundation of your small group.

Community. Small groups are a great place to develop deep friendships with other Christians. Allow time for informal interaction before and after each study. Plan activities and games that will help you get to know each other. Spend time having fun together—going on a picnic or cooking dinner together.

Worship and prayer. Your study will be enhanced by spending time praising God together in prayer or song. Pray for each other's needs—and keep track of how God is answering prayer in your group. Ask God to help you to apply what you are learning in your study.

Outreach. Reaching out to others can be a practical way of applying what you are learning, and it will keep your group from becoming self-focused. Host a series of evangelistic discussions for your friends or neighbors. Clean up the yard of an elderly friend. Serve at a soup kitchen together, or spend a day working on a Habitat house.

Many more suggestions and helps in each of these areas are found in *Small Group Idea Book.* Information on building a small group can be found in *Small Group Leaders' Handbook* and *The Big Book on Small Groups* (both from InterVarsity Press). Reading through one of these books would be worth your time.

STUDY 1. BE STRONG. EPHESIANS 6:10-13.

PURPOSE: To understand the nature of spiritual warfare and the importance of the armor of God.

Introduction. You may encounter a participant who has a difficult time understanding or accepting the evil spiritual powers that stand against a follower of Jesus. As a group leader it might be helpful for you to have some background understanding of Satan and the forces under his control. I have written a book called *Angels Around Us* (originally published by InterVarsity Press but now out of print; however, it's available on Amazon Print on Demand) that contains several chapters on the devil and the evil angels who follow him. Other resources that might help are C. Fredrick Dickason, *Angels Elect and Evil* (Chicago: Moody Press, 1995), and *Angels*, a LifeGuide Bible Study I have written.

Other participants may overemphasize the role evil powers play in the Christian walk. The fact is that Satan is a defeated enemy and we are no longer under his dominion as believers (John 12:31; Colossians 1:13). Satan's power should not be minimized, but we should not live in fear of him. Sometimes a difficult person in our lives is just a difficult person, not an agent of the enemy! As a leader you should be prepared to bring biblical balance to the discussion in your group.

Question 2. The word translated "struggle" in verse 12 occurs only here in the New Testament. It is a word used primarily regarding wrestling (the King James Version says, "we wrestle not against"), but it can have a wider meaning of a fight or a battle. The terms used to describe evil spiritual forces probably do not give us ranks of evil angels but are simply various terms that Paul piles up for emphasis and impact on his readers. These are personal spiritual beings seeking to disrupt and discourage God's people. The struggle goes on "in the heavenly realms" (v. 12), meaning the realm in which angels (both good and evil) operate—a realm that is real but invisible to us.

Question 8. If participants are unsure, suggest they reflect on how they have received strength from God in the past. They can also consider people they know who seem to be strong in the Lord and what they can learn from them. (Think about how the responses to question 9 fit with this question too.)

STUDY 2. STAY TRUE. EPHESIANS 6:13-17; 2 TIMOTHY 3:10-17.

PURPOSE: To be confident in God's truth and live out the truth more fully.

Question 2. An understanding of God's truth and a personal allegiance to it holds our spiritual armor in place; it is support for the core of our faith and life. Without the truth found in God's Word, our faith and life as followers of Jesus would fall apart.

Questions 3 and 4. The world around us tends to view truth as relative (what is true for you may not be true for me—or it is only true in certain situations). God, by his very nature, is the source of all truth and his Word is true (1 John 1:5; John 17:17); his Word is true whether I accept it or not. Jesus said, "I am the way and the truth and the life" (John 14:6).

We can count on him to be true and to speak truth in every situation and into every circumstance of life.

Question 5. If truth is foundational, our enemy will do all he can to deceive us, to lead us away from the truth of God and into the lies of the world. The "truth" the world feeds us always has to be filtered and checked by the truth of God.

Question 6. In Ephesians Paul sees objective truth as coming from God in the gospel (Ephesians 1:13; 4:21). And truth is to be lived out in our words and actions (Ephesians 4:15, 24-25; 5:9). Both right thinking and right living are crucial elements. Studying the whole book of Ephesians can help us understand how to live in the truth.

Question 7. We can trust Scripture as true and act on what it says because it is the product of God himself. Paul encourages Timothy to "live a godly life in Christ Jesus" (2 Timothy 3:12) and continue in what he has learned and believed (2 Timothy 3:14), even though he may suffer for it as Paul did. Knowing the truth of Scripture equips us for good works.

Question 9. Timothy learned the truth from his family as a child, and he continued to learn from Paul. We are called not simply to know God's truth but also to communicate that truth and implant it in others, particularly in the next generation—in our children, grandchildren, or spiritual children.

STUDY 3. BE ON GUARD. EPHESIANS 6:14; 1 CORINTHIANS 16:10-14.

PURPOSE: To discover how God's righteousness protects us.

Question 1. According to the *Dictionary of Biblical Imagery*, the breastplate was "armor covering the warrior's thorax, abdomen and back. It would protect his vital organs from deadly wounds" ([Downers Grove, IL: InterVarsity Press, 1998], 46). Isaiah 59:17 describes God as a warrior with "righteousness as his breastplate."

Question 6. If group members ask about Apollos, the larger context can be found in 1 Corinthians 1:12; 3:4; 4:6. The Corinthians were asking for Apollos to return to them rather than Paul. It seems that Paul did urge Apollos to return. But according to biblical scholar Bruce Winter, Apollos's response "suggests that Apollos has judged that accepting the invitation at this time would not be in the interests of the congregation, given the tension between Paul and the church" (1 Corinthians, *The New Bible Commentary* [Downers Grove, IL: InterVarsity Press, 1994], 1186).

Question 7. The commands are (1) be on your guard, (2) stand firm in the faith, (3) be courageous, and (4) be strong (1 Corinthians 16:13).

Question 8. You may want to bring notecards for this exercise. You could pause and do it at this point or come back to it at the end of the session as a way to close.

STUDY 4. STAND FIRM. EPHESIANS 6:14-15; ROMANS 5:1-5.

PURPOSE: To be grounded in God's peace and ready to share this peace with others.

Question 2. In Ephesians 2:14-18, Paul describes how Christ's life, death, and resurrection gives humans peace with God and also creates peace between different groups of people—in this case Jews and Gentiles.

Question 4. Anywhere peace is absent in our life—in our hearts, our relationships, our work place, our home—the enemy is at work.

Question 5. In situations of disharmony God calls us to rise to our feet and move forward in truth and righteousness against the devil, who wants nothing more than to rob us of peace.

Question 9. According to Romans 5, peace with God is one of the many benefits Christ gives us. In this secure relationship with God, we can be confident and hopeful no matter what we experience.

STUDY 5. STAY CONFIDENT. EPHESIANS 6:16; PSALM 18:6-30.

PURPOSE: To continue to grow in faith in all circumstances.

Question 1. Roman soldiers used two kinds of shields. The first was a small, round shield secured to the forearm with leather straps. It was used in hand-to-hand combat to deflect or block sword blows from an opponent. The second kind was larger and heavier and made of a solid piece of wood and covered with leather or metal. This is the shield Paul refers to here. The tips of arrows used in combat were sometimes wrapped in strips of cloth and then soaked in tar. Just before the arrow was shot, the tip would be lit and the flaming darts would be sent aloft at the enemy. The tar on the arrow would become flaming gel that would spatter on impact, sending bits of burning material for several feet. If the tar landed on the soldier's clothing or other gear, it could ignite a distracting and even debilitating fire. The shield covered in leather could be soaked in water before battle and would then extinguish the arrow or flaming bits of tar.

"The flaming arrows of the evil one" (v. 16) connects back to "the devil's schemes" already mentioned (v. 11). These might be temptations to sin, the attacks and words of other people, personal fear, doubt, discouragement—all planned by our spiritual enemy to destroy and defeat us.

Question 3. Some students of Ephesians think that the shield of faith that deflects or extinguishes these arrows of attack is the Christian's own faith and trust in God. Other interpreters think it rests more on the faithful character of God—Christians can rest in our trustworthy God to provide victory. Certainly, both sides of faith play a part in our spiritual battle. A possible follow-up question would be, In your mind, does deliverance rest more on the strength of our faith or on the faithful character of God, and why?

Question 4. I have heard Pastor Tony Evans make this statement on several occasions: "Faith is acting like it is so, even when it is not so, so that it might be so, simply because God says so."

Question 5. Possible approaches include adopting a new attitude, taking a specific step of faith, or initiating a conversation that needs to happen.

Question 10. An alternate wording for this question is, Do you find a greater emphasis in this passage on God's faithfulness or on our faith? Explain.

STUDY 6. BE ASSURED. EPHESIANS 6:17; 1 THESSALONIANS 5:8-11.

PURPOSE: To be confident in our salvation every day.

Questions 1 and 2. The purpose of the helmet was to protect the soldier's head (brain, mind, thoughts). Our enemy, Satan, will seek to use doubt, questions about the genuineness of our faith, and accusations about our past or present failures or sins to cripple us in battle.

Question 4. This is another opportunity for you as a leader to share some of the struggles and doubts you have had (or may presently have). You may have dealt with those attacks by claiming God's clear promises, by seeking spiritual advice from a more mature friend, or by putting that doubt under the light of God's Word and putting it to rest once and for all.

Question 5. Words like *vulnerable, careless,* and *unwise* come to mind. How would those qualities reveal themselves in the heat of spiritual battle?

Question 6. Each piece of armor is put on with accompanying qualities of self-control and spiritual awareness.

Question 8. Those in the body of Christ who are already armored and who have been through their share of spiritual battles are responsible to encourage and bolster those in the body who may be immature or shaken by spiritual attack. The Thessalonian followers of Jesus were doing exactly what Paul wanted them to do.

Question 9. This is a good question to use to probe the genuine commitment of those in the group to others in the group or their church. How effectively are we using our experiences and spiritual wisdom to help others who may be going through a time of attack?

Question 10. The helmet had to be intentionally put on. Ask the group for suggestions on how they can remember to each day put on the helmet of salvation in preparation for potential battle. This might include avoiding things that dull our awareness and distract us from the good things God has called us to.

STUDY 7. BE COURAGEOUS. EPHESIANS 6:17; HEBREWS 4:12-13.

PURPOSE: To understand how God's Word equips us for life and spiritual warfare.

Question 2. Earlier in Ephesians, Paul described how the "the Spirit of wisdom and revelation" helps us better know God and his truth (Ephesians 1:17-19).

Question 3. Craig S. Keener writes, "The double-edged sword (*gladius*, 20-24 inches long) was a weapon used when close battle was joined with the enemy and the heavy pikes that frontline soldiers carried were no longer practical. Thus Paul implies that the battle is to be joined especially by engaging those who do not know God's Word (the gospel) with its message, after one is spiritually prepared in the other ways listed here. Paul's ministry was thus particularly strategic, because it included close-range battle advancing into enemy ranks (vv. 19-20)" (*The IVP Bible Background Commentary: New Testament*, 2nd ed. [Downers Grove, IL: IVP Academic, 2014], 555).

Question 5. If group members don't have a personal story, an alternate question is, Give an example of a biblical account in which someone used God's Word to resist the devil. Let each person share their story (or biblical story) without judgment or correction from others in the group. The key biblical account of resisting the devil with God's Word is the temptation of Jesus in the wilderness, when he countered each of Satan's temptations with an appropriate quotation from the Old Testament book of Deuteronomy (see Matthew 4:1-11).

STUDY 8. STAY DEPENDENT. EPHESIANS 6:18-20; COLOSSIANS 1:9-14.

PURPOSE: To understand the importance of prayer and how to grow in prayer.

Question 2. The pattern of prayer in the New Testament is that we pray *to* the Father, *through* the Son, and *in* the Spirit. Romans 8:26-27 may help explain the phrase *in the Spirit* that Paul uses here. It means first that we pray for what the Spirit wants us to pray for. As we follow the Spirit's direction, we will have confidence that certain requests are in God's will. As a result, we will pray in faith. Second, to pray *in the Spirit*, means that the Holy Spirit provides the energy for our prayer. He empowers the discouraged and the weary. Some Christians take this phrase to mean that we pray in tongues, through the language of the Spirit. Do not let your discussion get bogged down on this issue. You may have some participants who assert this view firmly and others who do not think the gift of tongues is part of this discussion. Agree to disagree and move on. The important thing is that we pray in the Spirit.

Question 3. We tend to think of prayer in one way—making a request of God. But Paul opens the door to a whole variety of prayers. Maybe you could have tagboard, a whiteboard, or paper handy to list those kinds of prayers, such as confession, thanksgiving, intercession, adoration, praise, meditation, and humility before God. What about song? Crying out to God? Seeking after God?

Question 6. Prayer is not for God's benefit but for ours. As we persevere before God in prayer, we grow in our dependence on and faith in him. Time spent in prayer may also change the way we pray about a need or request. What we think should happen becomes instead surrender to the will and decision of God.

Question 9. There is no mention in Paul's prayer for anyone's sickness or financial needs or marriage struggles. That doesn't mean we shouldn't pray for those things, but there are other issues we should focus on more consistently—spiritual maturity, for example, or a heart of surrender to God's will.

Douglas Connelly (d. 2023) was the author of more than twenty LifeGuide® Bible study guides with over 200,000 copies sold, as well as a number of books. He was senior pastor most recently at Davison Missionary Church near Flint, Michigan, after serving twelve years as senior pastor at Parkside Community Church in Sterling Heights, Michigan. He was married to Karen, and they had three adult children and six grandchildren.

WHAT SHOULD
WE STUDY NEXT?

LifeGuide®
BIBLE STUDIES

Since 1985 LifeGuide® Bible Studies have provided solid inductive Bible study content with field-tested questions that get groups talking— making for a one-of-a-kind Bible study experience. This series has more than 120 titles on Old and New Testament books, character studies, and topical studies. IVP's LifeGuide Finder is a great tool for searching for your next study topic: https://ivpress.com/lifeguidefinder.

Here are some ideas to get you started.

BIBLE BOOKS

An in-depth study of a Bible book is one of the richest experiences you could have in opening up the riches of Scripture. Many groups begin with a Gospel such as Mark or John. These guides are divided into two parts so that if twenty or twenty-six weeks feels like too much to do at once, the group can feel free to do half of the studies and take a break with another topic.

A shorter letter such as Philippians or Ephesians is also a great way to start. Shorter Old Testament studies include Ruth, Esther, and Job.

TOPICAL SERIES

Here are a few ideas of short series you might put together to cover a year of curriculum on a theme.

Christian Formation: *Christian Beliefs* (12 studies by Stephen D. Eyre), *Christian Character* (12 studies by Andrea Sterk & Peter Scazzero), *Christian Disciplines* (12 studies by Andrea Sterk & Peter Scazzero), *Evangelism* (12 studies by Rebecca Pippert & Ruth Siemens).

Building Community: *Christian Community* (10 studies by Rob Suggs), *Friendship* (10 studies by Carolyn Nystrom), *Spiritual Gifts* (8 studies by R. Paul Stevens), *Loving Justice* (12 studies by Bob and Carol Hunter).

GUIDES FOR SPECIFIC TYPES OF GROUPS

If you have a group that is serving a particular demographic, here are some specific ideas. Also note the list of studies for seekers on the back cover.

Women's Groups: *Women of the New Testament, Women of the Old Testament, Woman of God, Women & Identity, Motherhood*

Marriage and Parenting: *Marriage, Parenting, Grandparenting*